RESPECT YOUR CHOICES
Finding Balance in Success

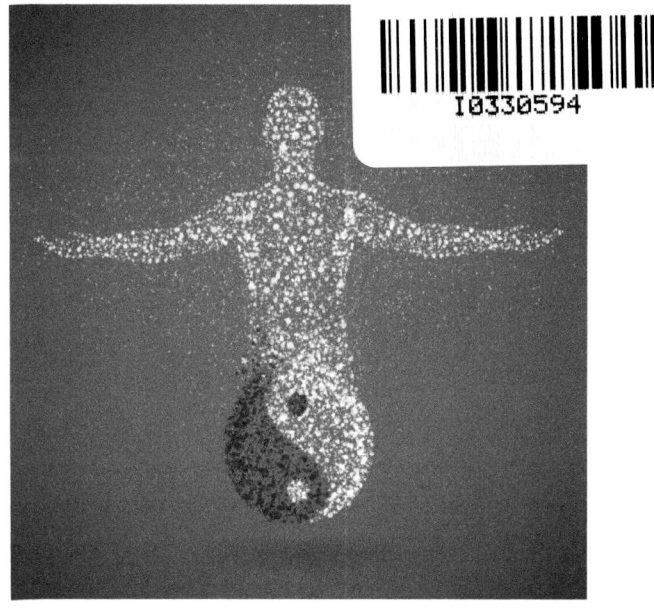

By
Vaughn J. McNeill

Respect Your Choices: Finding Balance in Success
Publisher: Pen Legacy Publishing
www.penlegacy.com

Respect Your Choices: Finding Balance in Success
written by: Vaughn J. McNeill
Cover Graphics by: Junnita Jackson

RESPECT YOUR CHOICES: FINDING BALANCE IN SUCCESS. Copyright © 2015 by Vaughn J. McNeill.

All rights reserved. Printed in the United States of America. No part of this book may be used or reproduced in any manner whatsoever without permission except in the case of brief quotations embodied in critical articles or reviews.

First Edition

Library of Congress Catalog- 2015918134
Paperback: 978-0-996-1880-2-9
Ebook: 978-0-996-1880-3-6

Table Of Contents

Dedication
1

Forward
5

Why This Book?
11

Live For Your purpose
15

There Is No Comparison
17

Purpose Versus Your Role
21

Respect
29

Respect Is Not Love
35

Respect Eases Fears
41

Respect Does Not Fear Society
45

Respect Change, Don't Fear It
49

Choices
55

Respect, Purpose, And Positive Choices
59

Knowledge And Choices
69

Choices And Relationships
77

Choices And Money
85

Choices And Perceptions
93

Success
99

Only You Can Define Success
101

What's Next?
105

Dedication

This book is dedicated to the one person I know, who lived their life according to their own rules, who embraced life and all it had to offer, who wasn't afraid to make choices, and chose to live it with as much passion and purpose she could muster!
Much love always Maria!

💬 *"Happiness is priceless, but you can afford it!"*
∼𝒱∼

Forward

You are the power source of your universe. Shouldn't you give power to everything and everyone in your life that provides you with happiness and fulfillment, and not to things or people that only bring you down and drain your power source? This can be as small as the words you choose to use to as large as where you choose to put down your roots. All things in our life require power to exist. So if you find you are powerless in life, turn the switch on for yourself and off for things and people not adding light, but rather constantly casting darkness. Negative situations and negative people require as much energy as positive people and positive situations need to exist. But it seems we spend a lot more energy on things that will not refuel our power source but rather empty it, and leave us feeling drained, resentful, and often times beating ourselves up. Why would we ever choose to beat ourselves up rather than lift ourselves up? If being negative uses as much energy as being positive, then why are so many of us making the choice to be negative? Why allow negativity to surround us, and choose not to embrace our lives, but rather what we think others' want our lives to be? We could choose to live life for ourselves and make choices that are positive and fulfilling, and decisions that will enhance us. Everything in our world starts and ends with the choices we make. Life is difficult on its own. Why must we insist on making it more complex than it needs to be?

To begin, let's start with defining and refining the words, "exist" and "life". Life is defined by Webster Dictionary as, "The sequence of physical and mental experiences that make up the existence of an individual". On the contrary, Exist means, "To have life or the functions of vitality". In other words, we must exist to be alive, but we must have our experiences, both good and bad, to LIVE! When you live life, you laugh, cry, hurt, and make memories and experiences along the way. You dance, sing, try new foods, learn new languages, take up crafts, or discover a new hobby. Friends and enemies are made, you make love, you argue, and you may or may not make up. Careers and jobs are started and lost, and you may or may not start a family. You may even decide to continue on with your education. I'm sure you understand where I am coming from. However, when you choose to only exist, you wake up to the same mundane, drab experience you call your life. Existing works for buildings, cars, books, radios, etc. They all exist. But do they live? Do they have experiences or memories? Sure they do in a weird way that we may not understand. But for the purpose of this book, no they do not! Existing does not work for a person wanting to experience life. I am not saying that existing does not work for some, because I am the first to say existing is relative. You, as the individual, should do what works for you. If doing things the same way all the time and never trying anything new works for you, that's awesome! Be that as it may, you may find this book does not focus on that point of view and also may not inspire you much, as it takes a certain mindset to want to live versus wanting to exist. A mindset of wanting to only exist will have you going through the motions of life without much regard to where you end up, how you get there, what drives your decisions, and who you choose to give your power to. However, you must ask yourself, "Why are you allowing yourself to only 'exist' when you have the choice to live life to the fullest, failures and all?"

Everything we do in life is based on a choice. Either a choice you make or a choice made on your behalf. It would seem very logical to assume most people actually thought about this fact and made as many positive choices for themselves as possible. Yet, far too many of us have no clue as to how much power we actually have over our lives, if we so choose to use it for us. So we allow ourselves to become drained of, and disengaged from it. It is easy to sit back and let others make decisions for you, but then you have to ask yourself, "Is it in your best interest to take what they offer or is it in your best interest to make your own choice?" Trust me, speaking from personal experience, it is much better to make the choices for yourself. When you make your own choice and that choice ends up being not such a good decision, it's much easier to forgive yourself. Or at least it should be! Allowing others to make choices for you can lead to a life filled with regrets and what ifs? It could seem that everyone around you seems to be surpassing you which may lead you to ask yourself, why? The answer may be because the decisions you are making are making them and their situation(s) better, and leaving you with nothing left to draw from. Furthermore, this can then lead you to making decisions that aren't really in your best interest. But then you discover you want to play catch up so bad, you lose sight of where you truly want to go. Making your own choices allows you to guide your life the way you feel it should go, take the paths you find interesting, and discover what you like or enjoy. *You* are the one that have lived and has to live with the choices you've made and will make, so why do so many of us continue to look for tour guides for our lives? Who better to guide you through your life than *you*? The best way to become that guide is to make choices that have positive effects on you and your world. Become your own navigator of life…

💬 *"Self-Respect eases fears life and society puts on us over time."*
~𝒱~

Why This Book?

  The hopes of this book, if you so choose, is that you transform, evolve, and progress in life. I believe we are all creators, our lives are the canvas, and our choices are the paint with which we use to color and shape our world.
  This book may help to show that no one can help you see happiness within you but *you*, as you have to choose to see it. Reading this book alone will not be sufficient to fully grasp the full purpose, as you will require action to see any change if change is what you are looking for. My intent is to have you think positively and change negative perceptions. If you change your perception, you change your outlook and once you change your outlook you change your outcome. Your outcome can be either positive or negative, as it's relative to *you*!
  There are many Americans who struggle with their identity and who have parents comprised of different races. Looking back, I could have let the fact that I'm biracial really get to me. Try walking around in a world that never seems to accept you. Try not fitting in because you're too dark to play with the white kids or too light to play with the black kids. Couple this with being adopted, the product of a broken home, living in the projects, and having no real role models. All the makings of a recipe for a disaster! Any of these events could have been reasons for me to give up, fall in with the 'bad crowd', and not look for or strive to reach my full potential. Furthermore, I could have been like the countless number of people that I have come into contact with that felt they

had no purpose or power. However, having experienced those situations firsthand actually left me compelled to write this book: Respect Your Choices! Finding Balance in Success.

I have met numerous individuals who have expressed sorrow as to how life has treated them. They may have been happy with some aspects of their lives, but as a whole, they felt incomplete and unrewarded. So I began asking questions, and with those questions distinct differences began to identify themselves. Both in those that weren't happy and not looking forward to the next day and those that were happy about and were eager to see what the next day has in store. Those that aren't satisfied with how their lives are going, more times than not, are not living their life for them, but rather for someone else. That someone else could be a parent, child, spouse, or friend. Even society will have you believing that you should live your life to please other people.

My plan is to engage you by asking challenging questions and offer self-provoking thoughts that may create a different thought process. You may begin to see who, what, and where the center of your life, happiness, and fulfillment begins. With *you*!

This book isn't designed to provide answers to an individual's life issues, difficulties, or problems but rather provide a different way at looking at those same issues, difficulties, and problems, and addressing them with a positive mindset.

💬 *"People will fight tooth and nail to keep things of little importance but freely give away the most precious thing they own -*
Their mind!"
~ V ~

Live For Your Purpose

What are you doing to enhance your life, purpose, or your future? This one question alone would take you a lifetime to answer as we are constantly doing something. However, ask yourself if what you are doing is hindering your process or helping you to maintain the status quo? While you think about that, let me ask you this. What are you doing to achieve your potential, your goal, and your destiny? The questions probably didn't get any easier, huh? But finding the answer is very necessary as you progress in this thing called life. Believe it or not, those questions seems to stump most people. Truth of the matter is, most people don't truly understand their true goal in life is to live the most positive and experienced-filled life possible. Being a good person and respecting yourself are things we all should strive for, that is, if we want true happiness, peace, and love. You need to understand that being the best person you can be is the only standard you should compare yourself too. Trying to live up to someone else's standard, or comparing yourself and life to anyone other than yourself, strips away your ability to experience your life. How can you reach your true potential, embrace and enjoy your purpose, or discover things that drive your passions, if you don't know where you started from, or which direction you would like to try next, if you don't know you?

There Is No Comparison

To honestly and accurately compare yourself to anyone else would mean you would have to make every decision they have made in their life up to the point you view them as a standard to attain. Not only would you need to have had the same outcome from the decision they have made, but it goes further, you would need to experience the emotional, physical, and mental impact those choices had on that person as well. Ask yourself is this even possible? I think you will agree with me in saying, NO! This is not possible! It *is* possible this may occur in some other universe, but definitely not here and now. Furthermore, if you have no chance of ever having the exact same outcome from experiences had by another person, how can you really think that someone else's life choices should be *your* life choices? Shouldn't you try to have as many experiences as you can in life? This does not mean you can't or shouldn't have stimuli. How else do we know about half of the crazy things we know to try? But that's all anyone should ever aspire to be to you, is an idea, a role model, or maybe the framework of the type of person you would like to be. But they should never be a standard or benchmark you feel you must attain. We must be true to who we are as individuals. And if you don't know, please use the words contained in this book as motivation to find out who you are and how you would like to be as a person. This means not who your parents think you should be, who your spouse thinks you should be, who your church thinks you should be, or who your children think you should be. Remember, you only get one life. But also remember, you have unlimited opportunities to make it what you need and desire. Therefore, you should not be overly concerned with what others may say because only you have the ability to live your life, and make the decisions you need to make for you. Once you start to let others define you, you become a victim of what I call, societal induced schizophrenia. It is possible you soon may begin to suffer from a clash of identities, thereby making it easier to lose yourself and your true life's purpose. This is because you have begun to live the life that others want for you, versus what *you* want for you. I am not saying not to have those people in your life, but do not let *their* pursuit of life and its joys overshadow your own. When you allow these different people to dictate your purpose, you allow them to define you. Will you choose to live for you and do things to ensure you have as a fulfilling and exciting life possible? Or, will you choose to live the life others' dictate to you? Who knows what's best for you besides *you*? Only you have walked in your shoes. Even if you were following in someone else's footprints, you had *your* shoes on. If the things you are doing do not enhance you or your purpose, and if you feel you are wasting time, you probably are! If you are having problems compounding your positive choices, chances are you aren't doing anything for yourself. You might be doing things for your parents, children, spouse, or even be doing things for your boss. But what about you? Realizing there is a balance in all of those things is ideal, but first you have to understand its ok that others may be sad, or let down by the choices you make. This is because everything is positive and negative and it may need to be bad for them at that moment for you to feel good. As long as you are not intentionally hurting people, you will be ok.

    Understanding life's purpose can bring you joy and can make the obstacles of life much easier to deal with. You may begin to see that everything in the universe has a place, and has a positive and negative, and in understanding and accepting this fact can make the hard times bearable and good times beautiful. Every decision made, every action taking, and every role in life, all have positives and negatives. You cannot have positive without negative, good without bad, and light without dark. It takes the opposite for the other to be true. The thing that makes this possible is duality and the need for things to balance out. As I mentioned earlier, what is positive for something or someone may not be so positive for something or someone else. For example, if you walk down the street and find a hundred dollars, that's a positive for you, right? But for the person that lost that hundred dollars, they probably would consider that a negative. Conversely, if *you* walk down the street and lose one hundred dollars, that would be a negative for you and a positive for whoever finds it. That's the natural balance of things.

While things must be good and or bad, we have the power to make the decision to see a problem as an opportunity. This is where people become labeled and or perceived as "successful", "getting by", or "unsuccessful". These labels can be extremely detrimental to the individual and their pursuit of their life purpose.

Purpose Versus Your Role

It can seem that your purpose is to be a parent, but ask yourself do you allow your children the chance and opportunities to explore and find their own purpose. Parents will always be parents and children will always be children, but what people forget to realize is that they are also individuals, with their own life, history, experiences, and decisions to make and to be made. You must not lose or permanently replace your life purpose with that of the purpose of being a parent. This is because those children will soon be seeking to make their own way, and see what they can create with their own color palate of life choices.

As children we had a better idea of our life's purpose, which was to live and enjoy life. It's only as we grow up and begin to deal with the consequences of our choices and those of others that we begin to lose sight of what life is meant for. The more responsibilities we assume or that are thrust upon us, and the more we begin to become other people for the sake of others, the further we get from our own happiness. If you think about it, you have to change and become a different person for each person in your life. You have to adjust to and become who they need or want you to be, thereby taking on another personality you have to maintain. If you allow them, each personality you assume for each person in your life can be perceived to be your purpose in life. Your spouse will need you to be a certain person, your boss will require you to be a different person, your children another, and your parents yet another. When you assume the role of providing happiness for others, *you* begin to change. That change slowly eats away at you and your purpose, until you no longer have an idea of your purpose outside of pleasing and doing for others. Assuming a role is normal, as you interact differently with each person. But what shouldn't be normal is you feeling those people and their happiness is now *your* responsibility. It can't be, and that's because each person chooses how they want to feel, and react to life. No matter how bad you want your child to go to college, if they don't want to engage in the process and take advantage, you will be wasting your time, energy, and money, in filling out the application, paying the tuition, dropping them off, etc. They have to want or desire the experience for themselves. Otherwise they will not do the work required for them to succeed. Remember, we alone are the power of our world. This holds true for you, your child, your mate, and every other person on this planet.

Your purpose should be to have the most positive life you can have for you. Each of these roles should be viewed as enhancements to your ultimate purpose, just like interest on your money in the bank. You would quickly withdraw all of the money you had in a bank, if they only charged you fees and never paid interest. If you hope that is not the case, why would you choose to continue to have people in your life that only take and never give? Why allow people to demand you be a rock for them, but they act like Jell-O for you? People will constantly lean on your for support if you allow them to. However those same people may not be a source of stability when you, yourself, are in need.

Your purpose isn't to wake up every day dreading some part of your life. Life isn't meant to be a negative. While there may be negative things that happen, life should be full of the experiences you *choose* to have. One way to see more of your purpose is to stop putting unwarranted obligations and expectations on others. The only person that is obligated or should be expected to do anything for you, is you. For example, it's not your wife's job to motivate you. It's not your husband's job to solve all of your problems. Nor are your parents obligated to help with your finances.

The responsibility of life alone is yours to bear; therefore, you must accept ownership and respect the responsibility of your own obligations. Embrace the freedoms and remember the obligations of being human. We should strive to be as positive and supportive to others as we would like them to be towards us. Everything in our worlds are connected to everything and everyone else. Each decision we make has an effect on someone else, even if you do not see *the* effect. Truly knowing and understanding this simple but yet very complex fact is key to finding your true purpose. It will help you understand that since all things are connected, all things must take place. Remember, everything has a purpose, both good and bad things must happen, and the good and bad aspect of everything is subjective to each individual person. Sometimes positive things happen for others and may not happen for you. This doesn't mean that you will lose out on life. It means that it is someone else's turn to gain a positive experience. Those roles flip from moment to moment, and accepting this is critical to having a more positive than negative life experience.

Since everyone on this planet has a purpose, and that purpose is to enjoy and have a positive life, you must accept that what may be good for your friend, may not be so good for you. Each person has their life to live and in doing so, will make choices that may affect your life in good or bad ways. You will have little to no chance of controlling things happening, or changing. The only thing you can and should control is yourself. In our lives, the best we can hope to ever control are our reactions to consequences of choices we do not like or understand. This is done by practicing self-respect, and understanding that your job right now is to enjoy and experience life as defined by you, not understand the why behind it.

Once you accept that everything has a purpose outside your perceived purpose, you begin to see purpose in both good and bad situations, and from that you can begin to shape your life in a way to enhance it. Think of this process like you are cooking. The smallest ingredients can have a huge impact on the recipe. Take for instance, adding salt to a recipe that called for sugar. This can ruin a meal. By changing one ingredient you may end up with a totally new dish. Using that same thought process, changing the way you think could give you a totally different outlook on life. A new outlook on life, could lead to a more positive and pleasurable life. We are all creators, and have the ability to create the type of life we wish to have with thought and above all ACTION!!!!!!!

Action is as important as any idea or thought. Without them both you are left out of balance. Action gives power to your experiences. This is true for wanting to live a purpose filled, fun, and fascinating life. The first thing is the thought, then comes the action. You will rarely succeed with a thought alone. Nor would you succeed in an action without thought. The action is just as critical as the idea, and the right action is essential. Where a lot of people go wrong is putting too much action into things that will not benefit them. For example, chasing the dreams of others or settling for less than they deserve because it's the easier decision to make. Wasting your most precious resources of time, energy, and ideas, etc. on people or things that will not enhance your purpose may prevent you from achieving just as much as if you never had the idea. This type of action can lead to you becoming resentful, less open to new ideas, new people, or any change at all.

People in your life should add value, and if they are not, why waste time, energy or thoughts on them? It's hard to do, especially if these people have been in your world for any measurable amount of time. But ask yourself, is their happiness worth more than your own? If you feel so, then my hopes are that after reading this book, you'll begin to see that no one else's happiness is worth any more or less than your own.

We shouldn't feel our purpose is to gossip and make light of someone else's plight or differences. Understanding that we all have purpose and that purpose is to live the best life possible means that we all have that obligation. It means make and capitalize on positive choices, because the negative actions will take care of themselves. This doesn't mean we are treating others badly. We should focus on making choices that will balance and promote our purpose and not hinder it. This becomes very complex if you are constantly looking at others as if they are better than you or beneath you. Comparing yourself to others you perceive as less than you is just as negative and unproductive as feeling you are deficient and less than someone you perceive to be better off than you.

Working towards your purpose may allow you to maximize your time, ideas, and it could also help to boost your self-esteem. Once you are able to see your purpose is to live your life for *you*, *y*ou will have a feeling of freedom, like the sky is the limit! This is because, as stated before, life is for living and not just existing.

Why choose to merely exist, or possibly worse, live for someone other than you, or spend your life in a state of constant comparison with anyone or anything other than *yourself*? You could just as easily choose to live for yourself, and make your own experiences, and not by trying to replicate another person's achievements.

Only you can live your life and deal with the consequences of your actions no matter where the idea comes from. Wouldn't it be in your best interest to make as many positive choices you can and make them based on where you want to be in life? Maybe not ultimately, but at least where you want to go next. If you don't know where you would like to go next, then *that* should become your standard of comparison. Ask yourself, am I in a better spot than I was a year, a month, or even a day ago? What you compare is up to you as long as you are comparing you to you. Are you in a better financial position than you were a year ago, or are you thinking about furthering your education? Once you begin to make understanding you and your purpose your goal, letting go of the previous standard of comparing yourself to others, can become as freeing as a life free of bills! If you decide to give it a try, what's the worst that can happen?

We all grow and evolve as individuals at different speeds and time. It may take me three times failing to learn a lesson my brother may have learned in one mistake. This does not make him better. It means that it took me three times and him one time to learn. Or, he may have seen a similar mistake made in the past. Or, he may have just been lucky. None of those reasons were for me to try and understand. What I must understand is me, and how can I take from each experiences I have in life, be them positive or negative, and apply those experiences if similar situation arise. I also must be proud of the fact that I did learn from that mistake and I can move forward in my life, putting it behind me. Doing so, I may be able to take advantage of the opportunities that may present themselves in the future. Life isn't a competition with society. It is a competition with *yourself.*

💬 *"It is very easy to lose your individual purpose when you are asked to assume roles or personalities for all of the various people in your world."*
~𝒱~

Respect

When I speak of respect I am not talking about yes please, and thank you. The respect I am referring to is the respect that starts with self, and how you choose to view yourself, and your surroundings. The respect you have for yourself has a lot to do with the happiness in life many of us are looking for. With a greater sense of self, you will be less likely to be drawn into traps such as comparing yourself to others, or settling for things, people, or situations that aren't the best for you. This is not a new concept. Respect for self and others in the world transcends time, culture, religion, as well as gender. This is why "The Golden Rule" has survived history, the rise and fall of civilizations, and continues to be the center of cultures today. Buddhism, "Treat not others in ways that you yourself would find hurtful" Udana-Vaga 5.38. Christianity, "In everything, do to others as you would have them do to you: for this is the law and prophets" Jesus, Matthew 7:32. Hinduism, "This is the sum of duty: do not do to others that would cause pain if done to you" Mahabharata, 5:1517. Islam, "Not one of you truly believes until you wish for others what you wish for yourself", The Prophet Mohammed, Hadith. Judaism, "What is hateful to you, do not do to your neighbor. This is the whole Torah; all the rest is commentary", Hillel Talmud, Shabbat 31a. Native Americans, "We are as much alive as we keep the Earth alive", Chief Dan George. Every culture and religion on the planet has a version of "The Golden Rule". It's what sets a path for us to follow, and helps to guide each of us in making choices that are not only positive for ourselves, but for every other person, animal, and plant on earth. Making positive choices will help to enhance the happiness and positive energy needed to continue to grow in acceptance and understanding of yourself and where you fit in this place called life.

Self-respect is key to living a happy and fulfilling life. With self-respect as your key, you can confidently open the doors of life, and explore various paths to the destination of your choice. Respecting oneself means knowing you have the right to happiness, and to pursue your life's dreams. Self-respect allows you the confidence to try new things, experience new places, and be more open to new ideas. As you go through life, understand that you will make both good and bad choices. But regardless the outcome of the choice, you are a wonderful person, and living life by taking chances, and making choices, the choices you make now are your memories for the future. Having respect for yourself will allow you to remove yourself from situations that aren't enhancing you or life purpose. Within self-respect you see that it's ok to fail, and to not reach the level you were striving for at a certain moment. Respect in yourself lets you see you are worth more than any success you have or seek to achieve, and that you're winning just by living life for what it is meant, to live! In living, you will have both failure and success. Don't forget, we cannot have one without the other, just like we cannot have good without bad.

Many people have heard the phrase "if you want better then be better!" However many struggle with the fact that being better is all part of a mindset. The good thing about it being a mindset is that it costs nothing to change. To change your mind is as free as the air you breathe. So if you want better or different you must think in a different and better context. In addition, ideas cost you nothing but can provide you with astronomical success. This is what makes ideas so priceless, the fact that they *are* priceless.

The main thing to keep in mind about "different" is that it does not always imply better. We cannot just say I want different for my life, because 'different' can be worse than the current situation. You have to want better *as well as* different, and having self-respect will dictate what that truly means to you. For example, having a job and wanting different could mean you have no job. I say this because we have to put as much thought into how we will execute change, as we do wanting the change itself. Wanting better, alone, is not enough. You must act upon that desire. Wanting without action is just more wanting. Just like knowing better is not enough. I know better than to speed but I slow down only when I see the police, is a good approach to take on the freeway. But knowing better and waiting for someone else to point it out in my life is a totally different thing.

Respect must first be given to yourself before you can truly pursue your life's purpose. Respect allows you to accept the fact that you are as special and as wonderful as any other person, and no one has the right to put their pursuits over the right of another person's pursuits. We all have dreams, desires, passions, hobbies, fears, regrets, and nightmares. That's what makes things so relative, the individualism of it all. But most of us have the ability to put ourselves in the shoes of each other if we so choose. Again, this makes the relative, relative to you. If we stopped and gave a moment of thought of how our actions would affect the next person, chances are we'd opt for a relatively positive choice. By not stopping and putting yourself in another person's shoes, it's very easy to lose sight of this common relativity and begin to think being selfish is the norm. It may be the norm for some, and in some cases it is ok to be selfish, but every action we make doesn't always have to end with us running around with raised fists, claiming to have conquered the world. We can get that same feeling by allowing someone else a chance to experience a win. This is not to say always put others' before you, because such behavior is not practical, logical, or anyway to live your life. But it is ok to allow others to experience a win. With respect for self, and the confidence to challenge yourself, you can define you, now, and the in the future. Without self-respect and low confidence, it will be very easy for you to allow others to define *you*.

💬 *"Respect will allow you to know yourself, and that the only boundary preventing you from success is your perception"*

~V~

Respect Is Not Love

    I will never say to love one's self if a person has not first learned to respect one's self. There are too many levels, aspects, and types of love for that to be the focal point of one's inner being.

    Let's explore the word 'love'. What *is* love? What is love to you? Why is it necessary for love to be validated? Just like many other words within the English dictionary, love is a word that is often taken out of context. Respect will allow you to understand that every person has their own purpose, their own ideas, thoughts, memories, and experiences, which makes them the unique, special, and the wonderful person that they are. Respect understands *they* may need to do things for themselves to fulfill their purpose and have their own life enhancements. This doesn't mean the person doesn't love you or have time for you, but merely they are trying to have an experience they choose to have and that experience may not involve you. Respect allows for trust, and trust allows for love to flourish. Now don't get me wrong. Love is a feeling of warm personal attachment or deep affection for something or someone. But what some fail to realize is that love does not supersede respect. Love and Respect, in my opinion, work much like a home. Respect would be the home, and Love would be the rooms of the home. The love for your children is different from the love you have for your parents, which is different from the love you have for friends, and different from the love you have for your significant other. Each of those people would represent the various rooms of your home. Your love for each room is different but the respect for the home should be the same. If you don't respect your home, how can you ask others to respect it and not take it for granted? For example, you can be in a serious relationship in which you love them and they love you back, but within that love should also live respect. Respect is the core of your love that should keep the relationship free from blemish or hurt. If you respect someone, you would be less likely to cheat, be abusive, or belittling. It's in the power of respect where you or your mate would reframe from any activity that could cause harm. Furthermore, if you are a parent, then you would need to respect the fact that your child has their own home, and will make choices that you may not like, but you would still have to respect that it's *their* choice.

On the other hand, love in its purest sense would embrace the hurting factor because it's simply an attachment or affection. Therefore, I challenge everyone to fully understand the power of respect when it comes to yourself and love before you jump into a love that is full of painful experiences. If you've ever been in love, then you understand what I am talking about.

I have seen so many people alter their whole life around for someone who claims to love them. They lower their standards and their self-respect just to say that they have a (wo)man. They lose their identity, their reality, and their self – love, leading them to now to be controlled by love. If the love is not mutual, what do you think will happen? The worst thing you can do for love is alter your life, lose it, and then get hurt because of it. If you had the clear understanding of respect, then it couldn't ever fully cause you to alter yourself to the point to where you are disrespected.

The rules of love lie within you first respecting yourself, setting the ground rules of what you will or will not accept, and maintaining that respect throughout the process. Love only works when respect is in the forefront of the situation. Respect takes the familiar use of the word love in the statement, "if you love me, then you would do this, or "if you love me then you wouldn't do that", out of your lexicon. If you respect them, you will know they have their own purpose and if they respect you they will know that you have your own desires, wants, and needs, as well.

Remember, love is an emotion that is always subject to change. Respecting that fact may help heal some wounds and prevent new ones from forming. I am not saying, don't love! But, love should come with a presence of mind that *the love* will require the respect of both people for it to always work.

How is that we often hear people say, "prove your love for me". But when was the last time you heard someone say, "Prove you *respect* me?" More than likely that's because respect is not something that needs to be proven. You're either respectful or disrespectful. And if someone were to say, "If you respect me, you would sacrifice your happiness for my happiness". You would probably ask them to kiss your ass! However, if the person asked you to prove your love, you may start to listen and thereby begin losing who *you* are. As stated by William James, "The deepest principle in human nature is the craving to be appreciated". People play on this belief and will have you losing yourself for love, because you are looking to be appreciated. Self-respect will allow you to appreciate you, where everything in your universe starts, instead of giving the credit to someone else.

We often look to make a difference in the lives of others, without first ensuring we are making a positive difference in our own lives. It's easy to see flaws and defects in others, because we can view them from the outside. Viewing ourselves, however, requires us to look at more than what we project for the outside world to see, but to look at who we truly are as a person. Not only who, but what, a human capable of amazing things, should we choose, and recognizing we do not need the backing of others to realize the greatness we have within.

💬"It is through loves painful experiences where we must learn that we have to first respect ourselves enough to not alter who we are for love or the thought of it."
~V~

Respect Eases Fears

Franklin D Roosevelt stated "the only thing to fear is fear itself." Your comfort zone is shaped and pad locked by fear. Believe in yourself, but don't become overconfident. You must find balance with this. Balance will help keep you grounded and may provide assistance with keeping you from overreaching and taking on more than you can manage alone. In addition finding this balance will help to boost and keep your self-confidence and self-respect high, which will help you identity potential windfalls and treacherous pitfalls.

You cannot live a failure free life. Trying to live a failure free life will have you paralyzed and stagnant for fear of making the wrong move. Staying stagnant brings its own set of perceived failures, so technically you *have* failed because you failed to try. You would be just as well off trying. At least in trying, you have an opportunity to succeed. In failing to move for fear of failure, you can miss out on numerous life opportunities. Don't fear the mistakes, as they are what allows each of us to appreciate the good times. Without failure how do you truly know success?

Self-confidence and a good sense of self, are vital if you ever hope to conquer one of life's biggest *purpose* thieves, fear! Fear is normal, but it should not paralyze you. Allowing this emotion to take control can lead to some of the biggest detriments you can inflict on yourself. For example, it could prevent you from finding your true life happiness, missing financial opportunities, and maybe ever finding true love. Some people have even had the laugh of their lives by overcoming a fear. Please remember that you should never fear living your life for you and your purpose.

As I stated a moment ago, you cannot live a failure free life. You should not fear making mistakes because mistakes are part of life, and they show that you are trying to live the life you want. It means you are not afraid to believe in the power you have within. This does not mean its ok to go out and make careless mistakes, as you should always look to make the best possible choice for you. To make beneficial choices, you must see that your greatness comes from within, and from within that greatness, you can bring out the power you need to help you conquer many of your life fears. Our internal power source is fueled by respect. The more respect you have for you then the stronger the source and more power you can tap into. Tapping into that power can help outshine the dark clouds that fear of judgment can bring into our lives. This is because the power of self-respect will negate much of the negative energy others project. You also can use that power to fight many of the fears of life, like rejection and failure. Having the internal power necessary, allows you to accept that you will make mistakes, but through mistakes made today, you are able to have a better tomorrow.

💬 *"Fear is not meant to prevent you from discovery, but allow for rationale thought that can often times result in opportunities of greatness."*
~𝒱~

Respect Does Not Fear Society

Respect for yourself, and self-empowerment, will also help you see the fears that other try to cast on you, are normally nothing but tactics of control. Consider some of the advertisements that attempt to sell us various methods of protection for ourselves, our possessions, and our loved ones. The message is always the same. Fear the burglar! Fear the fire! Fear your neighbor! Fear EVERYTHING!! But when you stop and look at what they tell you to be afraid of, more than likely it never happened and probably will never happen. Yes people are robbed, beat, and mistreated, every day. But those instances are only a small fraction of the interactions people have on a daily basis. Most interactions are done with respect for all involved. Often times in today's society, fear is only used as a revenue generator by business and others looking to profit off of negativity that fear inflicts.

I am not saying that bad things do not happen in the world and not to prepare for things that may happen, but how much is enough, and are you really any more safe by overlapping fears? Wouldn't your money be better served on things that bring happiness and joy to your life? Wouldn't your time and energy be better used on positive thoughts and actions that will enhance you and pursuit of your life purpose? For instance people will move to live in low crime neighborhoods. But that is not enough. The neighborhood they live in must also be a gated community, with constant security patrols and video monitoring. On top of this, they insure their homes and all of the property within. Then for added measures of security, many of these people add alarm systems with motion detectors and monitoring systems so that they can monitor their homes 24 hours a day, from anywhere in the world. Why in the world would anyone need to have so many overlapping measures of security? If you live in a low crime area, a gated community and have insurance, why do you need an alarm system? And if you have both insurance and alarm system, why do you need to monitor your home? You leave the house to get away from the house, not to look at it from afar.

If you think about it, the things often most valuable to you cannot be replaced, such as, photos, handmade objects, love letters, or things that illicit positive memories to you. A thief doesn't care about those things only what they can sell, and sell quickly. If you have insurance, you file a claim, and replace your things. What often puzzles me is why does society seem to promote this, as if we are best served being afraid! Society tells us we should want to live in a gated community, in a big house with cameras, to be afraid of your neighbor, or the man walking down the street. If you think about it, aren't we all the man or woman walking down the street? Aren't we *all* someone's neighbor? So are they saying we should be afraid of ourselves?

Wouldn't we as a society be better off, embracing each other and trying to find commonalities that we can build on, instead of identifying those differences in life that make the world what it is? One answer is that it provides them, society, with a means to take your power, keep you in line, and under control. They can play both sides and get nothing done, but their own agenda. It would appear that they want you to be content with blaming others for your perceived failures, but the deck is stacked against you. Unless you choose to educate yourself to all of the facts, those in positions of power love to use fear as a means of keeping you from educating, and empowering yourself. The only way to fight this is to choose to educate yourself with information that can make your tomorrow better than today.

The perception of physical harm, and loss of property, coupled with the fears of rejection, disappointment, disapproval, and failure has a lot of people, lost, confused, and looking to others to provide them with the answers that only they can provide for their own lives. Which often times, happens to be the direction they should choose to follow themselves in life, what they choose to do in life, how they choose to do it, when and where they should do it, and above all who they choose to allow in for the ride. In order to truly experience your life, you will need to be able to consistently ask and answer those questions for yourself. The more respect you have for you, then hopefully the better you will become at asking and answering those questions. Once we have that level of respect for ourselves, we can begin to show that same level of respect to all humans, and chances are, fear wouldn't be a revenue stream, but could be used to progress and move us all forward.

Fear is so powerful because it can present itself in so many different forms such as, fear of the unknown, fear of judgement, fear of failure, and or fear of success. Yes, people fear success as much as they fear failing. Why? Who knows, as each person will have their own reasons as to what they are afraid of, as well as why they are afraid.

One way you can help to control fear, is by expanding the ideas of who you are. This means not putting yourself, or better yet, your thoughts into a rigid box, where you are incapable of opening your mind to allow new or different thoughts to flow in. By believing in yourself and the power that resides within, you can begin to turn fears into challenges that you can overcome, and give you a few personal wins needed to fuel your machine of self-acceptance. The wins will also help to increase self-confidence, which in turn will help view other fears that may arise, as opportunities to experience the kind of life as you choose to have. To do this, we must choose to view the fears in our lives, as positive learning opportunities, and not as opportunities for rejection, disappointment, or failures that we try to avoid at all cost. The experiences and outcomes of tackling fears can be either good or bad. But regardless of the present outcome, you will have helped to add tools and skills to your 'life tool box' that you can use to build the life you want to have in the future.

We have to open our minds to many possibilities, because it takes many possibilities to make many realities. This means we have to understand that the world is much more than what we may see or even consider at the moment. Wouldn't society and you be better served by promoting education and not fear? Why not put the money into educating ourselves instead of scaring ourselves? Take the time and money spent monitoring your house and spend them on learning a foreign language. Who knows, once you are comfortable with the language you could then save the money for a trip to put into practice the language you learned.

Life experiences give us the armor we need when battling one of the biggest fears shared by most people on earth, the fear of change. Have you ever felt, or feel like a victim of fate, finding yourself drifting in an ocean of constant change that you have no control over? Do you find yourself going from lover to lover, job to job, or friend to friend, looking for some consistency in your life? If so, you are not alone. People often look to others, or things like job titles, to anchor their life to. If you don't recognize the true value of yourself, nor have self-respect, it will be very easy for you to float along in life, going where the current takes you or worse, picked up by anyone passing by. If you have respect for yourself, you will care where you end up, and more than likely, how you get there.

Hopefully, by now, you are beginning to see the importance of *you* setting the course for *your* own life, where *you* want it to go, and the experiences *you* want to have. Respect in yourself may help with the constant change that happens in all of our lives. It may be the map you use to fight through the waves of change, by setting a course for where you want your life to go and beginning to row towards it. The more positive experiences and self-respect you have, the easier setting your course would be, and moving towards it would be a lot more pleasurable. Going towards your goals and your purpose will allow you to follow a path you set for yourself, and not a path in which others tell you where you should be, or how they think you should get there. Once you have your course set and begin moving towards it, you will slowly begin to see that you're getting closer to your goal, and regain your sense of control and power over your life.

Respect Change, Don't Fear It

For a better understanding of change, you have to first realize that you cannot prevent change, so there is no need wasting your energy trying to. Try to align your goals with some of the currents of change, as some of the changes must be going your way. This will make working towards your goal much easier, and a lot more relaxing, as the change is doing the work for you. To take advantage of the currents, you should be constantly looking to enhance and expand your knowledge base, improve your skill set, and look for the positive in negative situations. All of these can most effectively be accomplished by respecting yourself.

Change is needed for progress and taking solace in that fact has helped me tremendously. You cannot progress without some measure of change. Think about it. A person trying to lose weight could not have lost weight without changing *something*. The thing that people want from change is for it to go in their favor. For example, not many people mind a change in their salary as long as it is an increase. The strife comes when that change is a decrease. With this being the case, why don't more people do things to help change go in their favor? Much of this is because most people do not see the change coming until it is time to change, and therefore, are forced to act. They do not see it coming because people lose sight of their self-respect, and begin seeing their life as a competition with the neighbor, or the image society says they are supposed to have because of skin color, gender, or lack of wealth. The list can go on and on. As I stated before, the only competition in your life should be *you today* vs *you tomorrow* and the tomorrow after that. This simple fact can help alleviate a lot of the things that blind us from our purpose; with one of the biggest being what others think we should be for ourselves and worse, for them. If you are constantly trying to be what someone needs you to be for them, how can you ever be *you*, or even begin to keep up with the change required of *you*? This will be one of the biggest storms of change you put yourself in, and if you are not anchored in who *you* are, you may find yourself blown all over the place, battered, bruised, and further away from where you were trying to go. Please remember, anchoring yourself in *you* will allow you to weather many storms of change, and will make it difficult for others to try and pull you off your course unless you choose to go in the same direction they are going.

Often times, you will find some of the most pleasant rides you have in life will be with new people or experiencing a new culture. Recall your childhood for a moment. Your curiosity was probably higher than it is now, and your acceptance of others was probably higher than it is now. Making friends and developing bonds were easier, and it was probably easier to remain happy and not take yourself too seriously. As a child, you allowed yourself to make mistakes because you believed with tomorrow, anything would be possible. You probably woke up greeting each day with anticipation for all the fun the day had in store. Why do we, as adults, not embrace that same mindset, and enjoy every day for what it is? Each new day is meant to make new friends, try new foods, go to new places, and explore the world. How come as children, we begged to go outside and play, wander the neighborhood, and search for bugs? But as adults, many are afraid to go outside, afraid to make a new friend, afraid to try new things, afraid to go to new places, and some are even afraid to explore their own neighborhood. As children, anything was possible, but as adults, we see everything as a problem. The only difference from our younger selves, in comparison to being an adult now, is our mindset, and thought process. Instead of seeing opportunities for fun, most often we see possibilities of failing.

To be different is to think different, and if you approach life as one full of opportunities versus one full of problems and complications, you will soon see that anything is again possible, and that you are that same super hero you were at 6! The younger you probably didn't fear change, but sought it out. The changes in our lives allow us to have new experiences. They can allow for new aspirations or dreams, and it does not always have to be negative. Remember, you may not be perfect at everything you try, but you're perfectly fine for trying.

Self-Respect may also help to alleviate regret in life, as it will hopefully allow most of your decisions to affect you in a positive way. If you are making decisions based on the direction you want your life to go, the changes that happen in your life, will often times work in your favor. This unfortunately can go the other way. What I mean is if you are making decisions in your life because you want to be like someone, you're trying to please someone, or you're trying to hold on to someone, then chances are, the changes that happen will not be in your favor. The decisions may benefit others, who in turn, may or may not help you. But that is *their* choice. Living life like this can lead to a lot of regret. And, as a result, can blind you to much more perilous changes headed in your direction. Knowing that life will present unexpected changes, it often perplexes me why people don't try to make as many positive decisions they can for themselves. It would seem it would be in your best interest to make the change that will happen, happen on your schedule, and go your way as often as possible? However, the standard seems to be, how can I make a decision so my parents will be proud of me, or my spouse will want to treat me how I want, not how *they* choose? How can I be me without fear others will not accept me for my choices? With such deep and life transforming questions, ask yourself how can you ever keep up with the changes that come with being a child, parent, spouse, employee, friend etc.? Shouldn't your standard be, how can I be the best I can be to me? Being the best you can be for you, may allow you the mental time needed to balance each of these roles, and make dealing with the changes that come with each role, easier. You may develop a better idea of your path at the moment, and in life as a whole. Again, once you know where you are going, it becomes easier to identify points of interest you may want to pursue.

The same respect you have for yourself, should be and must be given to everyone you interact with, that is, if you hope to have more positive than negative experiences along your life's journey. Doing this can reopen relationship doors that closed over the course time, or better yet keep them from closing to begin with. Respect can offer reassurances that there would be no reprisal from expressing one's opinion, views, or thoughts. By giving the same level of respect for our fellow man, as we have for ourselves, we as individuals will go a lot further in alleviating some of the biggest fears shared by all, the fears of rejection, and the fear of judgment. Without these fears, you could then be free to make the choices you see fit for you and your happiness, in whatever form that takes!

💬 *"How can you ever get ahead if you don't understand what is holding you back?"*
~V~

Choices

In life we all have the same number of hours in a day. It's the choices we make that seem to give some people what appears to be endless time, and others, not hardly enough. Each of us have the option to choose *who* we spend our time with, *what* we choose to do with the time, *when* we choose to use the time, *where* we choose to go during that time, and *how* we ultimately utilize the time. These things coupled with perception can dictate how successful or unsuccessful any moment in time will be.

Everything that is in our lives, we choose to put there. From the people we allow in, the job we chose, the food we eat, the time we wake up, to the car we purchase, is a choice. Meaning, we are the ones to blame if our life isn't going where we want it to go. We are also the ones to praise when our lives *are* going in the direction we want it to go. We can't blame anyone but ourselves for the choices we make, regardless of who or what we made the choice for. Is it your husband's fault that you did not finish your education because he felt it was better that you stayed home? Is it your wife's fault your credit is messed up because she didn't pay the bills? . Are your parents to blame when you treat people with little to no respect for them as human beings? I can go on and on about who is or isn't to blame for certain things. But it all ends up back at the same point. YOU!! Understanding one's role in life may assist in seeing that while you may create most of the problem in your life, you are also the solution to those problems.

In life, the best you can do is try to make positive choices that will benefit you now and in the future. However, making "positive" choices does not mean you will not make bad choices. But it should help to minimize and accept those not so good choices. Knowing, understanding, and striving for your goals in life through respect, may assist you in making choices that will help you get to where you're going faster, and hopefully with less stress and more happiness. The thing to always remember is as long as you have your power of choice, you can always correct any choice that isn't working, by making a different choice. Often, when we say a choice is hard, tough, or difficult, what we are really saying is that it's not that the choice is tough, but rather, the consequences and outcomes, are either not desired, or have far too many positives to choose from. Yes, that is the sucky part! But again, any choice can be changed by choosing something else. You never want to lose out on something because you were too afraid to make a choice. As we go through life, we try to make the best possible choice we can for ourselves. Well that *should* be the goal anyway!

💬 *"We often don't want to accept the fact that we play a major role in creating the problems in our lives."*
~V~

Respect, Purpose, And Positive Choices

Life is more than a collection of moments that make up *today*. Life is also, more than today, or at *this* moment. Life *is* yesterday, today, and tomorrow all rolled into one. The faster you learn or realize that yesterday affects today and tomorrow, the faster you can begin to make positive choices that may help enhance your purpose and your life. The choices we made yesterday have a huge impact on the choices we make today, and tomorrow. If you choose not to put gas in the car the night before, and then wake up late for work, your day might start off on the rough side. However, if you put gas in the night before, and woke up late for work the next morning, chances are you can adjust better to the day. There are a myriad of scenarios that make up your life. So I ask, shouldn't you try to make decisions that will benefit you not just for today but will also benefit you tomorrow?
The respect you have for yourself can help aid you in choosing how *you* define you. What does it mean to be (insert your name), and how does (insert your name) want to approach life? You can choose to go with society's version, your parent's version, your mate's version, or your friend's version, so forth and so on. But who has to live your life and deal with the consequences of your choices? Is it society, your parents, your friends, or your mate? Ultimately we, alone, must face the consequences of our choices, be them good or bad.

Just as we can forgive others for causing sadness or heartache, we should also have enough self-respect to forgive ourselves for choices we've made that may not have been the best choice to make at *that* time. However, far too many of us do not do that. We will forgive people for all kinds of behavior. Like making choices without giving much thought as to how *their* choices may negatively affect us. Alternatively, we won't allow *ourselves* the same luxury of forgiveness. Consider the following questions. If you can't forgive *yourself,* how can you respect *yourself*? Furthermore, if you don't respect yourself, how can you expect *others* to respect you? It's almost impossible to forgive anyone without respecting them. If you *truly* forgive someone, you have *some* level of respect for them. It often times seems as if we forget that we too are people, and are entitled to make choices that may not be best for us. The negative outcomes of those choices are the prices we pay for experiences, nothing more. The negative aspects of the choices should not be carried around forever because you've already learned from the experience. There is really no need in reliving it every day. Respect in yourself will help you see that you are more than the outcomes of your choices. Have I always had the understanding that I have now? No way! It has taking me years and numerous failures to reach this point of understanding and acceptance. And, I continue to strive to learn and understand more.

    What has helped me get to this level of self-respect, understanding, and acceptance at a fairly early age, are the number of life altering events I have experienced. I've had to overcome being adopted, biracial, raised by a single mother in poverty, and attend poorly performing public schools. In addition, I've been married, divorced, financially ruined (aka bankrupt), and homeless, all before the age of 25. I could have used any of those experiences to become resentful and bitter towards life. But that was not the kind of life I wanted for myself. Besides that, any of those situations could have been a reason for me to view my life as less than others. But I realized that is not true! I am just like you. I am worth as much as any other person on this planet.

    For me to begin to find self-acceptance, I had to understand most of those outcomes were the consequences of choices made by others. I realized, there was no need for me wasting time trying to understand *why* they made their choice. I had to look at how I was treating *myself*, and the choices *I* was making. I also realized that I was allowing others to make me feel powerless and down on myself. But why *should* I feel powerless? Why should I or anyone feel powerless when all we have to do is to choose to make more *powerful* choices? Then I recognized that making different choices would *first* require me to change the way I saw *myself*.

The first choice I made was to make my purpose be to try to live the happiest and most positive experience filled life I can for *me*. It would have been very easy for me to come down hard on myself, and pity myself, or begin to blame others for my perceived failures. I actually did for a while blame others for why MY life was not going the way I hoped, planned, or wanted it to go. I blamed my biological parents for not seeing the value in me; I blamed my adopted parents for not providing me with what I perceived as a good childhood. I blamed the streets for taking away people that I felt best knew me and my struggle. I blamed my wife, at the time, for not providing me with support when I needed it. I blamed the military for breaking me and then getting rid of me. I blamed the credit card companies and banks for allowing me the opportunities to put myself in so much debt. Then that blame slowly shifted to me and I wanted to know why? Why did all of these things happen to me? And why did the people in my life make the choices they made that affected my life so drastically? Then I realized, even if I found the reason why they made their choices, it would not allow me to feel better about myself. How could it be every person that I came into contact with had more control and influence over it than I had? Then it dawned on me. Trying to understand someone's choice is like trying to count the number of waves in the ocean. You may be able to do it, but is it worth the time and effort? For me it wasn't the best use of time, as I had already spent precious time chasing, and pursuing answers I really would not understand. As I began to ask these questions of myself, I had to look at the common theme, Me. I was affected by choices and consequences. But at the same time I had the opportunity to choose *how* I let those situations affect me.

I could have continued on the path I was on, which was getting me nowhere but where I perceived to be failure after failure. I began to see how I gave power to people and the affiliations they had. It was ME that allowed people to have that negative effect on me. So the same way I was choosing to allow others to have power over me, I had to choose to take my power back. To accomplish this, I had to understand that my life and its purpose was what I chose to make it, and not what anyone else wanted, planned, hoped, or dreamed it would be.

It would have been very easy for me to be upset about any one of the many choices made on my behalf, and sulk or be sad. It wasn't helping me to always see the dark in everything rather than see the brighter side of the situation. Taking being adopted for example, I could have said I'm adopted and I don't know where I come from or know who I'm related to? I could've questioned why I was put up for adoption? I could've continuously wondered if my birth parents thought of me. I could've wondered if the woman that just smiled as she passed by could be my birth mother. I also could've thought, am I just that bad of a person that my birth parents, the often labeled by society as being the "foundation, the future that our lives, are built on", abandon me? I could. But, why? What good would it do me other than reinforce the negative and counterproductive feelings that the situation brings. This thought process was not positive for me. Nor did it provide me with anything but feelings of remorse and resentment. This state of mind also made most of my relationships more difficult than they needed to be. I could not see the good in me, so how could others see the good in me. What I needed to do was to focus on myself, and what I could do for myself and not focus on what others didn't do for me. It was important for me to make choices that would make me happy. And I also had to choose to see the positives over the negatives.

After I began to focus more on my choices, and how the choices I made influenced my life, and that by respecting me and my choices, I could make choices that would allow my life to take a path that I wanted. However, with choices comes the possibility of change, and one of the best ways to benefit from change is to be open to change and understand that we can use all information we receive in our lives to make positive choices. We can make our lives how we want them to be. But we have to allow our minds to be free and open to new ideas and new concepts. This is how progress is made. And with progress, hopefully comes growth and understanding which can help you see that all things are possible.

You have to choose to keep an open mind, as it is very easy to allow your mind to close, especially if you choose to exist rather than live.

Our lives are comprised of nothing but the consequences of choices. Those made by us, and those made by others. All of the consequences of those choices make up our past, present, and future. Understanding and accepting the fact that you control your reality with the power of your choices, you can then choose to take part in those choices, or continue to have them made for you. Once you realize that the more positive choices you begin to make for *yourself*, you may then begin to see more positive opportunities present themselves to you.

Positive and negative both have their relative value, but for the sake of this book I will define positive as having a good effect for you and negative as harmful or having a bad effect. A positive choice for you means just that, a positive choice for you. Other people do not have to understand why you choose to make a decision that you think is best for you giving that the decision does not intentionally cause harm to others. This is because no one person's choices, desires, dreams, wants, should ever trump those of another. Regardless of how noble they portray their cause. Selfish choices and respect do not mix. When I say selfish, I am referring to the obliging, requesting, needing, wishing, or wanting someone to be the power source, from which you draw. This responsibility falls squarely on your shoulders, for only you know what truly motivates you and will get you to take the steps necessary to live the life you want. If you don't know what will motivate you, it may be you've been living a life trying to give others what you think they want, when you should be finding out what you need? What we all need is the time and opportunity to learn who we are, and time to become comfortable with the person we have chosen to be.

How could I find the time to understand me if I lived my life trying to understand the choices of others. This added no value to my life, and it stripped away my power of choice to follow the path I wanted to take for me at any moment in my life. I had to have enough respect for me and my choices that I didn't care if I was judged. I knew I'd be judged regardless if I did do something or did nothing. I had to have enough belief in me and my abilities that I didn't have to choose to live a life of comparison or have my main goal in life be to acquire as many "things" as I can to flaunt in front of other people who may not have as much as I have. I guess to some people it's easier to make others feel bad about their choices, so that they can feel good about their own choices, or lack thereof. That type of mentality clashed with how I felt on the inside. My purpose wasn't to make others feel inadequate in order for me to feel good. How could that be anyone's purpose, as it doesn't seem sustainable? Once there is no one around to fuel to the engines, what happens to the high flying jet? It becomes a heap of burning junk not many find any value in. No one to say, "Oh WOW!! I'm jealous"! No one to say, "I wish I were…." If there was no one for me to brag or boast to, what would then be my value?

What I needed to understand was why I felt the need to allow others to define me. Up until that point, all I knew in life was to try to get more money, attain some sort of prestige, and thought in order to be successful in life I needed to spend my life chasing the dreams of others. Why did I allow myself to succumb to allowing the choices of others define me? Why was I trying to fit into a mold, which was designed by others that didn't know me, or know what made me? Why was I wasting time trying to obtain what society says would make me happy?

The answer to those questions became easier, after I realized I wasn't showing myself much respect, nor was I permitting the choices I made for my life to actually guide my life. This is because I was choosing to give all of the things and people around me more of a commitment than I was showing myself. I was allowing their version or view of me to define me. I respected what they said about me more than I valued what I thought about myself. It wasn't until I began to give myself more respect that I realized how *I* was the one that defined me! The media didn't define me, the music I listened to, nor did the movies and television shows I watched define me. They were nothing more than forms of art or entertainment and nothing to try and mimic my life after. The images that family, friends, enemies, coworkers, and classmates had of me, were just that, images. Those images did not identify who I am, or what I may or may not want to be. Only I could define me and what it meant to be me, in my world. I recognized it was for *me* to determine:

- Who I wanted to be, at any given moment
- When I wanted to accomplish something by
- How I wanted to do what I wanted for me
- Where I wanted to be, and
- Whom I chose to experience 'it' with!

Once I made up my mind to start living life for my purpose, and making choices that would assist me in living in that purpose, and not allow other's to direct my life or define my purpose, the happier, understanding, and accepting of changes I have become.

💬 *"You may choose to be respectful. Or, you may choose not to be. Either way, It is a choice."*
~V~

Knowledge And Choices

I am sure you are familiar with the expression, "Garbage in! Garbage out! What you put in is what you get out." That concept can be applied to what we choose to learn. If you constantly fill your mind with negative thoughts, what can you hope to get from that input? The best you could hope for is those negative thoughts cause no harm, and worst could lead to you living a life deprived of options, and the inability to make use of the choices you make. On the other side of that coin, filling yourself with positive, constructive, empowering information, you could hope for new life adventures, and more positive experiences. You may discover new things about yourself, which you can then use to further enhance your life and the path you choose.

To take advantage of all this information and power, all we have to do is make a choice. The choice we have to make is to choose to remain positive, and choose to acquire knowledge and apply that knowledge to our lives. How much time are you spending reflecting on negative situations, outcomes, and experiences? How much further along in your life could you be if you spent that time on value adding activities like discovering, and exploring all life has to offer? As I continue to state, our lives are comprised of endless choices. The more educated we can become, the better choices we can make for ourselves and those around us.

Choosing to fill your time with things like stuffing your treasure chest of knowledge with useful and positive information versus keeping the box sealed or only allowing in negative information, can allow you to better benefit from those positive choices. It can help benefit by allowing you the ability to better plan for life, by providing you with the information, and experiences needed to align your wants in life with your needs. All of our wants and needs are on different scales, as the wants and needs are *relative,* to the person wanting or needing. For instance, a bigger person may need and want more food in a day than a smaller person. Both their needs and wants are the same in that they both want or need food. But the amount used to reach satisfaction, is what is different. Just like every other aspect of life, we all have different wants and needs. And to understand those wants and needs we need to understand ourselves. And to best understand ourselves we must know ourselves. How do you discover what your wants are if you refuse to open and let information in? You have the choice to keep what works for you, and throwing back what doesn't. But you can't exercise that option if you choose to keep your box closed.

    You may have heard someone say they are thirsty for knowledge, and if you offer to fill their cup with some knowledge they refuse to take the lid off, opting to go with saying, they don't think you are right. Chances are their cup is empty, or they do not want you to see that they are sipping on a cup filled with stereotypes, judgements, fear, and confusion. If they were sipping from a cup of true knowledge, they would definitely remove the lid, and welcome what you have to offer. They may challenge you with their own knowledge, and it is then, that bridges of understanding and acceptance can be built.

    Looking for the positives in your life can also assist with defeating the monster of boredom. If you find yourself saying how you are constantly bored, your life isn't where you want or hoped it would be like, more than likely you aren't doing much, and the things you are doing aren't for your own happiness. A lot of the boredom that plagues society could be rectified by exercising the right to choose differently. However, the main way to identify the different you want is to learn about all of your options. The best way to find out about all of your options is to open your mind to all possibilities via education. Keep in mind, formal education is not the only format for learning. You should look to learn from everything for the simple reason that everything is connected. But you have to be honest with yourself and understand you don't know everything, and you cannot possibly know everything. However you can choose to interact with people that do know more than you, and choose to listen and learn from them. There are countless ways in which you can find out about anything, the key is taking proactive steps.

> *"If you have the ability to read, you should never truly be bored."*
> *~V~*

    Reading provides you with ways to learn about countless options in life you may choose to find out more about. If you allow it, reading can possibly open the doors to communication by offering you the opportunity to learn a new language. In addition, it can provide information you can use to conquer fears that may be holding you back, such as the fear of failing. The fear of failing can be conquered by understanding what is involved in the choice you are afraid of making. Being knowledgeable of an endeavor can make the choice to try that endeavor easier, or the choice harder. Remember, that's relative to each person and that person deciding to make the choice. The important thing to understand is that acquiring as much knowledge as you can does nothing but add to your life, It may also make many of the challenging choices we face in our lives easier to make.

    I am not suggesting that reading alone be the means to easing boredom. But allow it to be a tool you could use to pry open the box of stationary comfort in which you may reside. You also have to follow up the acquisition of knowledge with the power of action. Just learning by itself doesn't make it useful. You must choose to do something with the information, otherwise its nothing more than just information. If you choose, you can use reading to discover places that may interest you and then visit them. You could learn about and then explore new foods and cultures. You could find out about an activity you may have always wanted to try, or something you may have just learned about. After you learn about it, find where you can have the experience, and go find out if it's something you could pursue or not. One of the objectives of life is to create as many positive memories and experiences as you can for yourself.

Why would you choose to hold on to wives tale, and labels rather electing to find out the facts from the source? Wouldn't we be better served making choices that will add value to our lives rather than making choices to maintain the status quo? For example, today, it is common knowledge that the sun rises in the east and sets in the west, and that it is the earth that rotates around the sun. However when that fact was first presented it was met with resistance, so much so that people were put to death for saying that the earth revolves around the sun. Had the people back then had the ability to communicate with others on the other side of the earth they would have known that the earth does indeed revolve around the sun, and those people may have lived to make other discoveries. I'm not in any way suggesting that you go as hard as to sacrifice yourself for a choice, but we should try to approach life with that same since of openness, and understand everything we see is not the way it has to be. We can see that we all have the capacity for greatness, regardless of your race, or gender. Numerous stereotypes continue to be broken. Americans use to think that blacks, and women did not have the mental capacity to govern themselves. Had we still held to that belief there would be no women, or blacks in positions that require them to not just govern themselves, but to govern an entire nation. Most things in life are difficult to learn until you begin to learn them. Learning the alphabet was difficult, until you practiced it. Learning to make positive choices for yourself, is a skill that many of us need to learn.

Educate yourself but learn the facts. You wouldn't ask your mechanic how to bake a pineapple upside down cake. Why take advice from people in the same boat as yourself? Meaning if your girlfriend is constantly struggling financially, she may not be the best person to consult on such matters, especially if you are making life changing choices based on *her* input. Why would you take advice from your friend, parent, or any relative that for one, has as much as or has less than you, or two, are asking to borrow money from *you*? One answer people give for making those choices, is they don't know better, and feel they don't have time to know better. I have an answer to that. And that answer is, go find out what you don't know. You may say, how do I know what I don't know? Well then, start there! And learn everything you can about everything you can. What are your interest? What have you always been curious about? Find out how the banks are able to take your one dollar deposit, and loan out ten dollars. And if you're asking is that true? Yes it is! Find out your credit score. If you're renting, find out how you can become a homeowner. Inquire into how your city, town, borough, or state, operates its budget and how the decisions made by your local lawmakers will benefit you. Or, do a search on the programs out there to help you find out what you don't know.

Knowledge comes in various forms. But its up to us to choose to see the value in the experience, situation, or outcomes that makes it practical and useful. We often times walk around with our internal power on low and self-respect light on dim, through negative action, and then wonder why we are in the dark. Allow knowledge to be the fuel you need to kick on the power switch to high. This may allow you to be more confident in your interactions with others, and may make dealing with those negative people and situations, easier.

💬 *"Knowledge is the one treasure that will never decrease but only increase in value."*
~𝒱~

Choices And Relationships

Increasing your knowledge base, and spending time looking for positives could be beneficial by allowing you to create positive interactions with your family, friends, and colleagues. This is because people like to gather, converse, and share experiences. Instead of following the norm of negative gossip because it's easy, try injecting some positives into the conversations. If it isn't well received, don't let that deter you from staying positive, as your positive vibe will attract other positives. Your circle should not be one that promotes constant negatives, as all of that negative energy just goes around and around, spreading to each member of the circle. This helps none in that circle, nor does it promote a since of pride in one's self. How can it if your circle sits around judging others outside the group, and worse yet, members inside the group for no reason other than to make themselves feel better? How, when you are constantly in unhealthy competitions with those that are supposed to be the closest to you, even if it hurts you financially, emotionally, or physically? When you have people in your life that are constantly negative, you slowly begin to absorb that negative energy; this is especially true if you do not think highly of yourself. If your circles contain only negative people, sorry to inform you, but you are more than likely also a victim of that negative energy. More than likely when you are not around *you* are the subject of discussion and likely you are the target of the group's judgments, ridicules, or the subject of the latest gossip. Those that need their identity and self-worth validated by others, really aren't happy with themselves, and they will do anything they can to prevent anyone, including themselves, from seeing that fact. How fun is it to associate with someone that only defines themselves by making you feel crappy about what you have, who you choose to love, where you choose to go, how you choose to live your life, or why you made the choice you made? You would probably say it's not much fun hanging with those types of people. If you have people in your life like this and they are not trying to help you get anywhere you want to go, that's probably because they need for you to stay on the same level as they are, in the hopes that you will continue to push *them*. Why choose to have these people in your life, for the sake of saying you have a friend, or a companion? You could just as easily spend the time you spend on addressing *their* needs, on finding and addressing the needs you have to make your life the way you want it. What would you be losing by eliminating people that only take from your life, and don't add value? You probably wouldn't be losing much. But chances are, you would start to have a life filled with positive experiences.

    If you are reading this and thinking this sounds familiar, then you may want to consider new circles that will encourage you, and not degrade you or anyone else. Promoting positivity and uplifting one another should be the goal when deciding on the next circle you join. In your search for more positive circles, you will need to be receptive and able to see people for who they are, and not who you think they should be. Who says you can only have people in your circle that look like you, think like you, or have the same beliefs as you? Does it matter if your circle consists of a Chinese cowboy, a Rastafarian Eskimo, or any other combination, as long as they respect, support, and encourage you to pursue your own positive goals? The statement: "you have to earn respect", in my opinion, is way off base. This statement is all wrong because respect should be given freely. How it is that people have to earn the respect of another before they are not stolen from, lied too, or abused? The list goes on and on! This type of logic makes no sense to me. What should be earned is love, trust, and admiration. But respect, that should be given right away. Respect should be common amongst all of us because we all have the same worth and right to live life as we choose. We all have the opportunity to live a happy life, as we define it, so long as each of us respect the rights of others.

    Much too often we make choices based on the wants and needs of others, but the consequences of those choices do nothing but hurt us. For example, you agree to give a friend a ride knowing that you only have enough gas to get you to work. But they asked you for a ride and being the good person and friend you want them to perceive you as, you agree. If you get them to work, and they don't offer to give you gas money, and you choose not to ask, then you are just as wrong as they are for not offering. How were they supposed to know your situation? If you did not get to work on time because you ran out of gas, then you are as much to blame. Actually, it's all of your blame to carry. In this situation, you would have had plenty of opportunities to make your choice work for you as the person you choose to help. There are countless choices and options for that to work in your favor. Being honest, and saying you don't have money for gas might have been the best option. But the fear of being judged creeps in, so you keep quiet. Why, when the judgment of running out of gas and being late for work, will probably be just as embarrassing? Plus, why would you feel bad when they are asking *you* for the ride? You could have offered to take them part of the way. You could have said that you are unable to meet your own obligations and assist them too. Any of these choices are yours to make and you would be within all your rights to just say no with no explanation. If they aren't ok with that, and demanding you put their needs before your own, then you may want to look at making different choices as to who you let in and offer help to.

    The way you choose to respect yourself has a huge influence on how others will choose to respect you. The more respect you choose to show yourself, the more you can demand others show you that same level, or not be in your life. We should strive to give others the same respect we have for ourselves. However if we have no respect for ourselves, then how can we ever truly respect others or expect others to respect us? It's all a two way street. We all have to give to receive. When a person gives too much or others receive too much, then the relationship becomes out of balance. It doesn't matter if you give more than your receive, or receive more than you give. It's out of balance. Finding the right balance may help make the choices you make for you a lot easier. There may come times in dealing with others where it is ok to give a little more, or receive a little more, but that should never be the crux of the relationship. This isn't limited to a romantic relationship, as the word relationship can be "the way in which two or more people are connected" as defined by Webster Merriam. This would mean all of the relationships you have in life should be treated with respect and balance. Anytime things are out of balance, you can and more than likely, will have serious problems. For instance, if your car tires aren't balanced, you can cause serious damage to your car, your body, someone, or something else. The same can be said for your life. If your life is out of balance, you may have the same dangerous problems of hurting you, your life, someone else's life etc. Much like your car tires though, life can be easily brought back into balance, and that's done by choosing to always respect yourself and others.

It's easy to ask someone to examine the people in their life and adjust accordingly. But let's try it the other way. Look at *your* life and the people you have in it and consider the following questions:

- Are you an asset to the people in your life?
- Do you enhance their purpose?

Honestly ask yourself, do you ask them to "change this, change that"; "don't do this, do that"; "I need you to do this" or, "I need you to do that", without stopping to think how these types of statements could effect a person? Does what I am asking for coincide with their wants, or needs? Is it even feasible for me to ask this person for this? How would I feel if I were them? Asking yourself these questions or similar ones, will give you an idea of how the person views you. With this, you can use the answers to adjust your relationship with the person, hopefully for the better. We often do not pay attention to the role we play in the relationships we have with people. We sometimes are the ones to sabotage friendships, familial relationships, or romantic relationships because we fail to see how *our* demands affect others. People become so preoccupied with *their* wants, needs, and desires, that they forget they are not the only people affected by their actions. For us to all experience peace and harmony, we need to understand that our individual pursuits', should never supersede those of anyone else. Either demanding that someone give up their own, or put them on pause for you, is just as bad as that person were asked to give up their individual pursuit of happiness for someone else. We all deserve that, in whatever positive capacity that means. But not one of us, are more important than the other.

Choose to perform at your highest at all times, but do not expect that other people will share your level of performance. This sounds like a negative thought, but trust me that's ok, because actually it leaves room for nothing but surprises, regardless if they are pleasant or unpleasant. The unpleasant surprises can be just as much a win as the pleasant ones, especially if you choose to learn from them. You may see the pattern again later in life when the loss would be much greater. You may be able to assist a friend or family member that is going through same experience, but it's all in how you choose to view it. This doesn't mean going out looking for negative relationships, but rather to understand that bad things happen, in the course of two people on different paths meeting. It's like literally two worlds colliding. How can there not be any unpleasant events. If Earth was to collide with another world, most would expect the Earth to be damaged. How can we interact with others and not expect to have some damage or negative experiences. Without the negative relationships, how do we know better?

Choosing to show respect does not mean that a person will return the respect being given. If they do not afford you the same level of respect as they are being shown, then they are not worth your time and you can then request they regain your respect. If there are people in your life who choose, to not show you the level of respect you feel they should, you need to first ensure you are making that choice for yourself. Are you giving yourself the level of respect you are asking of others? Just getting rid of someone that isn't showing you the respect you feel you deserve will not fix the problem, especially if it's you that has the problem with respecting you. Once you are comfortable with respecting you and the value you possess, you can then begin to choose to allow others in; with the expectations they treat you as you choose to treat you. If they are choosing to not show you the same level of respect that you show yourself why are you entertaining them? Is hanging out with them the best use of your precious time? If after that, you conclude they are not the best use of your time, get rid of them until they decide too, and if that is never, what would you be losing? Too often we do things for others without much regard to how those actions will affect us now, and in the future. A true friend or someone that wants you to succeed will want you to make the best choices for you, without regard to how your choice will impact them. Those people that only concern themselves, with themselves, are people that you may not want to associate with, as their selfishness, can be detrimental to you building the positive life you want for yourself.

If you think of those negative people in terms of investments, spending time on them would not be a good investment. So why continue to feed it? Why would you continue to give someone a dollar if every time you gave it to them, they threw it away? If that happened, you probably wouldn't give them any more after the first. And, with that being the case, why allow or continue to allow, anyone to remain in your present, that doesn't choose to respect your future?

The faster you can see that you choose who you let in, the faster you can get through the screening process of who would best be suited to remain in your world. This means the people you choose to let in, must choose to respect you, regardless of their relationship to you. If you think about it, it should be the closest people to you that show you the most respect, but often times they are the ones choosing to show you the least amount of respect. Please know, it is ok to not have those people in your life until they choose to see you as the person you are choosing to be.

If you are following your own path, setting your own trends, making your mark on the world, you really do not have time to bring negativity to someone else trying to set their own trend, or make their mark. Negativity may always show itself, but intentionally sabotaging someone else's life, for your enjoyment, or for you to feel is your only way to get ahead, shows no thought on your part. We should strive to support and build each other up, not tear others down, because of fear, jealousy, or for any reason, for that matter. We should see the power in all of our differences. We are all unalike for a reason, and each difference allows for new opportunities and discoveries. Having respect for yourself first will make it that much easier to accept, and maybe understand these differences. We should embrace each other and our differences. Often times, the ideas of others may be a source of energy you would have never thought to tap into. By doing this, we can compound on the success and discoveries of others, and thereby enhance our own lives, without doing twice the work. This is one of the powers of positive choice. If the choice is truly positive, it will help and benefit far more people than yourself and your immediate circles.

Without a good sense of self, and with low self-respect, it becomes easy to put yourself in situations where you do not see your value. So you may, at times, devalue yourself, for the sake of someone else. Society tells you that you shouldn't be alone, but then it's, you shouldn't settle. Or we hear, you have to be married with children before a certain age, or you will not meet the 'status quo', definition of being successful in romance. Are you in a romantic relationship because of convenience and or, obligation? Do you feel the person you're with, is the best you can do? An even better question to ask is, why *is* the person choosing to be in relationship with you? Is it because you're the best *they* feel they can do, that they can get everything they need from you, that they feel obligated, or are you just there to pass the time by? If you do not know the answer to either of these questions, I would highly suggest you give the questions further thought, and then, discuss the answers with your partner. If you are in a relationship for any of those reasons, or any reason other than, the person balances you and brings you more happiness and positivity than negativity, you may want to reconsider who you are with. You must be honest with you and your partner, if you hope to find that magic that love is said to bring. The people that you let into your life have so many influences on your life. They are on your mind even when they are not in your presence. Since they will be in your thoughts, wouldn't it be in your best interest if they gave you more positive thoughts than negative thoughts? If you are worried about them cheating on you, them not working, them not helping with the household, worried they're not pulling their weight, or wonder if the house will be clean when you get home, or if the bills were paid, why allow them to take up so much of your time and energy on negative thoughts? Wouldn't life be happier if you had thoughts of I love and how you and your mate communicate? How much brighter would your day be if that person brought a smile to your face at the thought of them? Life may be less stressful if you knew that you can trust that they will handle their responsibilities, and not leave them for you? You can never reach a level like this if you aren't honest with yourself, and the person you wish to have in your life. But above all, they must respect themselves as much as you respect you. If not, you will have a relationship out of balance, and as I keep stating, balance is critical to happiness. The person or persons you choose to have in your life should add as much value to your life as you add to theirs and only those involved in that relationship determine what those values are. No one else!

Choices And Money

The reason I am talking about money and choices is because so many people say they *want* money, want to be rich, want to travel, want the newest clothes, the fanciest homes, and the fastest cars. But when I ask them how they plan to obtain these things, they have no idea. They know nothing of their credit scores, or about ARM's and I do not mean the body parts! They have no tangible assets, other than the clothes on their backs, which they often sell. This tells me that they really don't want what they say they want, because if you want something for yourself, why would you let anything or anyone, stop you from obtaining it? You would do the work required to reach the goal. The same way you can set a reminder to watch a show that will more than likely, not add value in your life, you can set a timer to learn about a company you might consider investing in. Instead of you and your friends talking about what so and so wore yesterday, why not form an investment group and talk about a stock's performance, versus an entertainers' performance. I am not saying not to have fun. Enjoy what you like! But remember you must find balance because, balance is critical to happiness. Like most things in life you must find balance. For example, let's use the example of saving your money and spending your money. If you have hopes of having a positive present and future, balancing these two are pivotal in achieving that goal.

My life, like many, has been filled with numerous setbacks, complications, pain, loneliness, and despair. Not too long ago, I subscribed to the mentality that a lot of people endorse now. That being, I will have bills until I die, so there was no need to plan for anything other than to make enough money to pay bills and live it up. This was great for a while, until life does what it does best, it changed! With this change came the big realization that I wasn't as set as I had set myself up to be. I had platinum credit cards, a new car every year, and new clothes every month, all giving it no thought because I knew I could afford the monthly payments…until I couldn't! The next thing I knew, I was 23 with 2 children, had a rocky marriage, and one hundred and eighty thousand dollars in debt, with no house and no other real assets. This began a spiral that included me filing for bankruptcy, becoming homeless, and completely lost in life. I didn't even have a bank account, after all of those things happened to me. At my bankruptcy hearing, the judge looked at the amount of debt and my age, and took pity on me, and discharged all of my debts. This was a break I needed to take full advantage of. It was up to me to make better choices about my money. Not doing so could result in me being in the same position later in life, where starting from scratch would be a lot harder. I had to learn how to better manage my money and life, otherwise I would continue following the path that lead me to file for bankruptcy in the first place. Or, I could take a different path. The choice was difficult, especially because many people in my circle at the time did not understand my goals or plans. I told myself the next 23 years would have to be better, as I felt completely discouraged, and stupid for getting myself into that position. These feelings only slowed my progress, and recovery. They prevented me from seeing or acting on opportunities, as I was afraid of making the same mistakes. I began to see all of my life as a "failure" and the negatives in my life where that much more highlighted and often seemed insurmountable. It wasn't until I accepted the fact that I made mistakes, and would make many more in the pursuit of my dreams, that I couldn't continue to beat myself up over decisions that I made. We all make mistakes. What makes my mistake or your mistake worse than others? Nothing does! So with this thought and the choice to learn from the mistakes, I began to my build and climb my ladder of positivity, and out of the hole of negativity I was in.

How you choose to handle or manage your money in today's society is just as crucial as how you manage your time. Try to make the choices you want not for today, coincide with your wants for tomorrow and each tomorrow thereafter. To manage your money you must know how to manage your money for you, and in order to manage your money, you must educate yourself about your money. Learning how to manage your money doesn't mean reading a book on investing, watching a financial television show, talking to one financial planner, or only putting your money in the bank. It requires all of these actions and more. It requires thought, planning commitment, and a desire to set and strive for goals. Only you know what you want your financial status to look like. You are very capable of defining how much is enough for you, as you are ultimately the one that has to live with your choice. However the power of choice allows you to change the goal as you see fit allowing you to stay flexible. Being flexible will allow you to better adapt to change, and to take advantages of changes rather being a victim of the changes. Again above all, it requires you to take a proactive role in managing your money, and to go beyond the mentality of, how much is my check, and how much can I spend? How are you trying to get ahead if year after year you're doing the same things that got you nowhere in previous years? It takes more than telling people how great you can be if you tried. You must actually choose to act on the actions you talk about, otherwise it's just talk. If you claim you could make a million dollars if you wanted to, then why don't you? Is it the million dollars you desire, or is it the attention you get from telling people how great you could be if you tried?

   Reaching the comfort level you desire will require you getting uncomfortable. Often times I hear, how do I take advantage of change, and how can I get my money working for me, rather than me working for my money? The answer is, you cannot, when you have never been educated, or took the time to educate yourself on money and how it works. You can't buy into other people's views or opinions, unless you want their opinion to be your own. For instance, I hear people saying things like, "people like us don't invest in the stock market", or, "we will have debt until we die!" And, they say things like, "that's for rich people!" But in the same sentence state how they want to be rich. This makes no sense to me, so they want to become wealthy, but do not want to do take advantages of opportunities others did to become wealthy?

For this process to work well, you will need to figure out how you can use the information you learned today to make tomorrow and day thereafter, better than the day before. Everything I listed before, reading books, talking to financial planners, and watching television, are all choices. You have to choose to see that you have the ability to do anything you want if you truly want it. It appears many people are more content with talking about what they would do if they had more money, than they are with doing the work required to obtain more money. They would rather spend more of their time marveling at the money other people have, rather than discuss how they can seed their own money tree. Information is at our finger tips, should we choose to capitalize on it. I am sure you have seen a person, and wondered how they are able to make choices for their life, such as, buying the car they want, with no worries. You may think, what do they have or do that I do not have or do? What are you doing to get the income or wealth you desire? Are you marveling, hustling, or a combination? What are you doing with your time?

Why do people spend so much of their time discussing their favorite television shows as if that is the only thing that matters in their life and then complain they cannot get ahead? Why do they discuss sports as if they are the owners of the teams, and they have control over what player goes where and when? And, asking how much money does this person make, vs someone else? How does any of this help *you* in your financial goals? The only purpose of television shows, and sporting events are to entertain you for that moment, not consume your entire day. How can you obtain *Power*, or build your own *Empire* if you don't make the necessary choices that will maximize your time and efforts? We can't wait to get to work to talk about the show and what the characters said. On our break, we watch recorded episodes, and when we get home, we turn on entertainment TV to find out the latest gossip about the actor. Then you are talking to your significant other or friends about the show when you get home. How does any of this help you? I only used those shows as they seem to be some of the more popular shows on television. But you can substitute any show, or any activity, in which the only benefit you get from the activity is entertainment. How does committing most of your time to one or several activities that do not add value to your life, provide you peace of mind? Wouldn't getting your finances to a level where you can begin to enjoy more of the options life has for you, be wonderful? If you are living check to check, how does spending all of your free time on things that do not improve your financial status, benefiting you? Are your activities working to provide you with the mental peace of knowing that you and your family will be provided for? Even if you are not living paycheck to paycheck, does it make sense to spend TIME, which is the most precious thing you have, on things that will not benefit you? Entertainment does add *some* value, but you can't retire by watching Game of Thrones because you're not building a valuable return on your investment, nor by spending most of your time digesting the stats of your favorite athlete. Use your power of choice to help find balance between things that entertain you and things that will provide wealth enhancement in your life. Choose to see that you cannot spend all of your money, and you cannot save it all. Doing either exhibits extreme behavior. As I have stated, you need balance, and being extreme on either end does not bring about balance. Remember, you must find balance by putting yourself in situations *to* win, and by taking advantage of all of your opportunities and resources.

    It takes money to make money, so if you are always spending it on things that will not add value, then you may have missed out on opportunities that would have the money, work for you. On the flip side, if you are always saving your money, how are you enjoying the benefits of your actions? This does not only apply to wealthy people. It applies to *all* people. If you don't have as much money as you'd like now, then don't save as much nor should you spend as much. But doing something small for yourself often, will reap the same reward as doing something big for yourself every once in a while. Meaning, if you can afford to save, invest ten dollars a week, then you save that, until you're able to save eleven dollars. This works a lot better than, "Oh! I will put two thousand in the bank when I get my tax return". When you get your tax return, how likely are you to save, or invest vs spend it? Saving the ten dollars a month may give you a sense of accomplishment, which is important in continuing to make choices for yourself, because you would immediately see the benefit.

If your choice is to work for others, then you must continually do things to ensure your value is known to them. You can't just settle in a position and hope that you can ride a wave of success to the top. The waves of success are created by you. They are created by building networks, continuing to further your education, or identifying problems and offering suggestions on how to fix the problems. Doing these things may help you get where you are trying to get to, in lieu of sitting around gossiping, or complaining that you can't get ahead. You have to want to improve your situation, and then do the work required to get you where it is you want to go.

If you feel stumped in life and do not see many opportunities, you can try looking for opportunities in the solutions to many of society's problems. For instance, you could look into starting a recycling center, getting politically involved in your community, starting a community garden, a book club, or an investment club. If you live in a city with abandoned lots, go find out if the city has incentives to be rid of the deserted buildings. There may be a program where you could purchase the lots for only the back taxes due. I mentioned investment clubs earlier. This could be a way that you get your friends and family exposed to stocks, bonds, real estate trust, and other financial vehicles. Doing any of these activities during your free time, could add value to your current situation, even if all you gain from it, is knowledge. You could accomplish multiple goals, be in a better position to recognition potential problems, and ultimately have a solution to remedy negative situations. By solving some of society's problems, you can find a solution you may be able to use for yourself, you could increase your wealth, make your community better, or whatever you feel would be a positive outcome. Remember, knowledge is a treasure no one can take from you.

💬"You cannot obtain wealth by being afraid of it, especially if you have to build it yourself."
~V~

Choices And Perceptions

With the power of self-respect and a different understanding of your life purpose, you can begin to choose how you want to perceive the world and your place in it. You can choose to perceive it as full of wonder, exciting new possibilities, opportunities for growth and enhancement, or you can choose to view it as stale, old, boring, and monotonous. You could choose to view it as dangerous, scary, and overwhelming, or you could see it as full of pleasant surprises, and electrifying moments.

How we choose to perceive the world plays a huge part in how the world perceives you. You control your perception of the world, and everything in it. And with this perception, you have the ability to exert a lot of influence over your overall happiness and pursuit of your life purpose and passion. What gives perception so much power is its ability to be unique to the perceiver. This allows it to change at any moment. This also allows you the opportunity to see things how you choose to see them, and not how anyone else views them. With this power, you also can choose to view your world and life as wonderful things to embrace and enjoy. You can choose to do everything for someone. However, they may not view your efforts in the same positive light. They may view your effort as negative and a hassle. Who would be right, them or you? You both would be right, and wrong. You would be right, but your perception may not be shared by the other person. But then you be wrong if you didn't respect the choice of the other person's perception. With that being the case, how can anyone's perception outweigh that of someone else? If no one's perception outweighs that of another, why allow someone to interject their negative perceptions, into your positive world?

With the power of perception, we have the ability to turn many negative life situations into positive experiences. To do this, all that is required is to change your mind, and mindset. This simple task however is extremely difficult for many people. It seems they get stuck in one frame of mind and are unable see any other possibilities. Why would anyone choose to limit their life options by closing their mind to other thoughts or ideas? Why would anyone choose to perceive themselves in any light other than a positive light? It appears to me that people do this because it is easier to see that the failures of the past become part of the the known. Meaning only seeing negtives in a very weird way, becomes part of the comfort zone that many people choose to reside. This comfort zone soon becomes the norm, not just for the individual but for society, as each and every one of us make up our society. Why shouldn't looking for and capitalzing off of the positives we find, be the norm? I think if we come to grips with the fact that many of the negatives we dwell on, are only the consequences of others pursuing their purpose, we can make this the norm. This is because, as stated before, trying to understand why a person makes their choices is not the best use of time. However, choosing to look for the positives can allow time for finding things that will add value to your life, and also help you identify both new and beneficial ways of delaing with similar negative situations, if they arise.

    You have to choose to stay decidated to perceiving life as positive, as it doesn't require much effort to slip into the hole of negativity. In my opion, one of the biggest reasons people choose to only dwell on the negative, is because they feel the negative comfort zone they reside will somehow prevent change. The world around us changes constantly, and being upset that things will not remain the same will only leave you bitter and possibly missing out on a life full of happiness. People often pereive change as a negative, but remember everything must be both positive and negative to remain in balance. So while some change maybe negative, it may be needed for progress.

    You can captialize on change often by staying positive. For instance, you can view losing a job as a negative or a positive. Viewing it as a negative may have you dealing with mental and physical stress. It may have you settling for any job that comes your way. I am in no way saying that you should walk around thinking everything is sunshine and puppies, because thinking that way, is unrealistic. You can balance out the negative with positive perceptions. Yes it may be bad to lose a job, but it could also be an opportubites for you to start your own business. Or, it may lead to a similar position with higher pay. The position may have never been known to you had you remained employed, but this type of thought requires effort. This mindset requires you stay positive more than negative which can be a daunting task in todays society. With the powers of perception and choice, you can choose to perceive life not only as negative, but also see that there are as many positives in life as there are negatives. If we all made that choice, we may be able to choose to see both positive and negative events are needed for balance and use this fact to shape our lives in the ways we want our them to go.

💬*"It seems people choose to remember the negative yesterdays because it's easier than choosing to create a positive tomorrow."*
~V~

Success

Now that you have reached this chapter, you should actually be proud and ready to activate your journey with the information learned. Let's take a minute to recap. We first discussed your purpose and the importance of knowing and understanding your purpose and how only *you* control it. And, that others do not have to understand your purpose, but they must respect *it* and *you*. We then went deeper into helping you understand the power of respect and why having respect for self is critical when it comes to making positive and hopefully life enhancing choices. In addition, we showed the power of your choices and the need for you to respect your choices. And to conclude, the last chapter introduces *success* and how you and only you define your success at any and every moment. Before you can truly define success, you must understand how finding balance in your purpose, finding balancing in respect for you and for others, and finding balance in your choices, plays in that definition.

Only You Can Define Success

There is no blue print to follow to succeed in life. This is because success is relative to the individual. Yes there are things in today's society that represent success. However even those definitions change with time and thought. Let's take a look at what is listed as the definition of success. Success is defined, by Merriam Webster, as "the fact of getting or achieving wealth, respect, or fame". We can see that respect is a form of success, so if you have respect you are successful. And on the opposite side of that, if you do not have respect that would make you unsuccessful. Please keep in mind the respect I am referring to does not come from anywhere but from within you. You must respect yourself first and foremost, and if you have self-respect you have already begun to succeed. Use this success as your platform to build on. As I have said before, doing so will help you to compound your successes.

We all deserve the right to live the best life we see fit for us, and become what we define success to be. This means we have the right and obligation to live up to only our expectations and definition of success. We are not to try to live up to someone else's definition of success. If you perceive yourself to be a success, you will always be a success. But if you are trying to be what someone else perceives as successful, you don't have that same guarantee. Success comes in many variations. That's the beauty of it. It can be anything from getting straight A's in school, to becoming the world's richest person. What makes you a success in life, is you living your life for you and having as many positive experiences you can. How can anyone define another as a failure? How can someone walk into a room and say, because I chose to be janitor, I am a failure, or not successful? Who is to say because you choose to be a teacher instead ofq being a rap star, you have or have not succeeded. When did stepping on your fellow man to get ahead become the standard for a "successful" person? What happened to being a good person? Are you not a success if you contribute to society instead of taking from society? The question of whether or not you are a success is one only you should answer for yourself. Only you know if you are going through life giving your all, and making the best of all of your choices. This is one of the true measurements of success. Are you happy with you and how you have lived and continue to live? Remember, trying to achieve someone else's version of success, may lead to temporary moments of success, but if you are not doing things for yourself in those moments, they will be short lived. You will then spend time trying to figure out why you are not content and then realize, it could be very well that you are not happy because you are not striving for your definition of success but for someone else's definition.

You have the choice to perceive yourself as what success means in your world. All of us have that power. Your version of success should not be what you hold others too. We must understand that we all have different levels and measures of success, and that each is just as valid and creditable as any other. We all cannot and will not become millionaires, so why is this the measure of success or ultimate status? Are you saying you are not successful at life because you have not accumulated enough money to go and buy out the mall? Am I not successful, if I do not have multiple houses and numerous cars? I can only live in one house at a time and can only drive one car at a time. I thought the American dream was up to the individual, and what we choose success to mean.

If there is something you truly want, what do you allow to stop you? For almost every instance the only thing that stops us from anything is *us*. Most of us are stopped from greatness because we choose not to look for it, and we choose to go along with the status quo. How easy is it for you not to realize your potential if you never see it in yourself? If you are constantly looking outward to find value, when do you invest in you and become the success you choose? As I stated, life is nothing but choices, those we make and those made by others. Therefore, it is imperative that for you to be successful, you must choose to perceive yourself as a success. Success does not come without "failure". Remember you can't live a failure free life, and failing does not mean you are a failure or unsuccessful. Failing means you thought enough of yourself to try, and for trying you are automatically winning. If you are winning, then you must also be a success, as success is another word for victory, but you have to see it. You have to use your power of choice to choose to see past your previous setbacks, and obstacles, and view yourself as a success. You have all the power you need to make any endeavor you take on successful, because again, only *you* determine when you have achieved your goal.

If you allow yourself to be coaxed into believing that your success is measured against anything but you, it's easy to get you to chase whatever standard someone else says you are supposed to measure up to. For example, viewing yourself as unsuccessful, would then make it easy for someone to have you degrade yourself, or allow them to abuse you mentally and or physically for the sake of being successful in love. It may have you thinking to be a great employee you will stay and work past your shift, and accept less money. It seems like society is becoming the defining measurement of success and not the individual person. Shouldn't your measure of success be based on your individual needs, wants, and desires, and not what others say you should want or have?

What defines success to you does not have to make sense to anyone other than you, as only you live your life, and have to deal with the consequences of your choices. The same philosophy can apply to all of us. We have all lived our lives and gained experiences based on the choices that we made. So who better than you to define what success means to you? If success to you is paying your bills and living a life of solitude, that's successful. If success means making a billion dollars, or starring in a movie, that's success to you. However please keep in mind these definitions of success are no less successful than someone defining success as living their dream of being a farmer. That's the great thing about success and it being relative. You can choose to define it however you want.

One way to reach your goal of success is to always look to make the most of every minute you have. Why wait until the end of the year to make a new resolution to improve, and or enhance your life and its purpose? You can make a new resolution every day, every hour, every minute if you so choose. The latter might get quite confusing and complicated, but hey, it's your choice! Wake up with a new resolution to learn a new fact each day, resolve to break free of a closed minded mentality, challenge yourself, and realize, you are your true competition. Recognize the greatness within. If you don't know how, then try. Give yourself a daily goal, and tell yourself you are proud of you, once you accomplish that goal. Expose yourself to new experiences, try new things, take a pottery class, and try a new food once a week. Try starting out small and build on each success and achievement. For example, if you want to lose weight, plan to walk an extra 500 feet today, 505 feet tomorrow, so forth and so on. With each of these mini achievements, you will begin to see that you *do* have power to control your life and how it goes.

Remember, by building on each success, you can compound on your positive choices, and make life begin to do what it does best, work for you. This concept is similar to gaining compounding interest, where the more you earn in interest the more, you EARN in interest. By doing this you can maximize all of your choices, and by maximizing your choices you can maximize your time, and by maximizing your time you can maximize your happiness. Life wants you to achieve and succeed, but you have to do your part, and your part is doing something more than wait for it to fall into your lap.

What's Next?

We have arrived at the part now where you ask yourself, what's next? How are you going to use the respect for you to make choices that enhance you and your purpose? What actions are you going to take now to define your success? I will tell you this, regardless of the choices you make, if you make them with respect for yourself and those around you, chances are you will win more than you lose. But please keep in your forefront, there will always need to be balance in your life. Finding balance is a great way to see that we all win and we all lose. But with the power of choice, you can *choose* to succeed more than you fail!

What will YOUR choices be?

ORDER PAGE INFO

Please visit www.Amazon.com or vaughnjmcneill@gmail.com
For autographed copies or bulk and special orders,
please email vaughnjmcneill@gmail.com

www.ingramcontent.com/pod-product-compliance
Lightning Source LLC
Chambersburg PA
CBHW070542300426
44113CB00011B/1757